ANCHOR BOOKS

INSPIRATIONS FROM

THE SOUTH WEST

Edited by

David Foskett

First published in Great Britain in 1996 by
ANCHOR BOOKS
1-2 Wainman Road, Woodston,
Peterborough, PE2 7BU

HB ISBN 1 85930 330 7
SB ISBN 1 85930 335 8

Foreword

Anchor Books is a small press, established in 1992, with the aim of promoting readable poetry to as wide an audience as possible.

The poems in *Inspirations From the South West* represent a cross-section of style and content.

These poems are written by young and old alike, united in their passion for writing poetry.

I trust this selection will delight and please the authors from *the South West* and all those who enjoy reading poetry.

David Foskett
Editor

CONTENTS

CANDLEPOWER

How nice it is to be without
Electric light - a noisy shout;
But candlepower, like early sun,
Calm as still mist - it's floating on
The air I cannot see or hear
- Only the candle's flame so near,
And moths may burn their dusty wings;
- In the kitchen, the kettle sings,
But not quite modern, such a thing,
Far off days remembrance will bring
On Autumn nights, of much delight
Of mellowness within my sight;
That mellowness of past ages
As I turn the yellow pages
Of a book,, where I have written:
'Man cannot from light lie hidden!'

Jon M de Joux

THOUGHTS ON THE SEA

Waters lay deep along shores
Untouched by man till those early ships:
Romans at Richborough when Claudius came to extend Gaul,
Then quiet Celtic monks and turbulent Vikings.
Men rode more upon the sea
Until they sailed the world
Leaving from Plymouth town and London's murky light
To find new lands:
Islands of spice, shining El Dorado
And America's green-leafed shore.

This day by Trevose the sea moving
Slowly washing sands washed eternal.
Though high tide be near the sea so gentle
That rocks of heavy seaweed sleep
Beneath unbroken waves.

The calm deceives:
Yesterday the high granite cliffs
Were torn and blasted by a fearsome tide:
Gulls hid trembling in caverns dark
And the wild chasms of the ocean thundered and were rent:
In Padstow boats and limpets clung fearfully to grey harbour walls,
Unearthly the cataclysmic light pierced
The swollen, uncontrolled night.

Alan Cave

ABBEY IN THE EICHWALD

The graveyard settled in the mist
Deep in a fearful vale,
Where no-one treads in day, nor night
Fearing what may prevail.

Foreboding, black, wrought iron gates
With age, they are decaying,
But still keeps shut, from centuries past,
To stop stranger steps from treading.

Bindweed traps the railings,
Moss suffocates the graves,
The graveyard surrounds the abbey,
Which in the vale it lays.

The mist, a vapour blanket cold,
Hangs low o'er hills and vales,
The solitary building, centuries old,
Stands high, from within the rusting rails.

Upon a bleak and windy night
The old, cracked bell may toll,
And knell the passing of an age,
And every long, lost soul.

E Richmond

VAMPIRE LOVERS

He came that night
      soft and quiet as the drifting snowfall
that lay heaped against the window
- bringing with him all the aching release
      that I longed for -
and as I fell with him into oblivion
the moths brushed our lips with their dusty wings
drawn by the twin suns glowing deep within us.

This delicate love,
so much stronger than the frailties of human passions,
    binds us together
    beyond undeath
and now I am sated on the fruit of ultimate knowledge;
    its chalky skin giving way to deep red flesh
    and flooding my mouth with its juices.

Can there be anything more than this -
    cool moonlight and your mouth
        against my neck?

I can feel your need
and as my blood flows with yours
we travel through my veins
    drinking from the chalice of
      the only true communion.

Viki Holmes

MOONLIGHT BLUE

I lie alone in this bed still tainted with your memory
Inside four walls which silently witnessed every scene
In our cheap soap opera romantic comedy
Cold reminders of the way things might have been

As I disinter dead fairy tales of yesteryear
Through the endless sleepless hours of the moon
Can't help but recollect a time when you were here
But now I'm just alone here in our room

The pillow that I rest on doesn't look right to me
It looks too empty, too cold and too bare
Without the moonlight through the window shining free
Upon the sleeping cascades of your flowing hair

And if these walls could speak, the stories they could tell
Of all the lovers' secrets that they keep
But I remember it all far too well
Too well to find a sanctuary in sleep

But when the morning comes then I'll miss you the most
I used to face each new day by your side
Tomorrow I can't wake with my arms 'round the ghost
Of all the love that went away and died.

Keith Bowden

ST MARY'S EWSHOT

We walked the last remaining yards
My little lad and I.
Looked down the hill, the cottaged road,
Green fields to pale blue sky.
We placed our bikes by the open gate
And quietly entered there.
A sanctuary of stone and mossy mounds,
Neglect and loving care.

We stood before the solid door
My little lad and I.
And as we pondered what to do
We heard the faintest sigh
Of voices murmuring indistinct,
Yet somehow very near.
Should we go into this place
Or quietly disappear?

We walked all round the stoney walls
My little lad and I.
To seek the source of sounds so strange
And our queries satisfy.
Yet all the while the murmuring
So soft but very clear
Echoed from each single stone
And teased my questioning ear.

Irresolute upon the step we stood
My little lad and I.
In spite of curiosity
We had no wish to pry
Perchance some rites were taking place
At this odd time of day.
The urge to enter too, was strong -
But we might be in the way.

Enticing sounds invited us
My little lad and I.
Perhaps the oaken door was locked?
At least we could but try.
I turned the ring with gentle care
For fear of too much din.
I had no wish to startle those
Who murmured there within.

We softly pushed the portal wide
My little lad and I.
Light filled the empty silent church
And then, as in reply
To unsaid thoughts, I felt a voice
That stirred within me say
'The souls of those who've gone before
Have called you in - to pray.'

William E Stimson

YOU'LL BE LUCKY!

You pick up a slip from the counter,
Mark on it six striking black lines,
Pass it back to the smiling assistant,
She's seen it so many times.

Sit down in front of the tele,
Watch Anthea dance a routine,
Hope Mystic Meg mentions your star sign,
Clasp hands and pray for your dream.

The celebrity pushes the button,
Then Arthur starts to spin 'round,
You sit there in absolute silence,
Afraid to utter a sound.

The balls drop into the channel,
Each announced with joyous abound,
But a quick glance down at the ticket,
Confirms that yours aren't around.

So there's no celebrating this evening,
No joy at a large jackpot win,
You stand as you screw up your ticket,
And curse as it lands in the bin.

But forget it all for an instant,
The fact that the kids need to eat,
Take your last coin and scratch off a ticket,
Another Lottery weekend complete.

P R Stananought

FLORIDA

The stars are out in Florida,
It's a dream that holds them there;
The sun dries out your sadness,
And the sea soothes all your cares.

Turquoise and golden shades,
A perfume to the air,
Atone for brawling traffic,
Like dodgems at the fair.

Escape from harsh realities,
Bring your fantasies to share;
At the end of the I. 95,
Paradise is waiting there.

Geoff Mourté

THE SEA OF LIFE

Three words
We've grown apart
you were my anchor
you were my base

There is nothing to
hold me down
to keep me safe
in the sea of life
I feel all alone
there's no private island
in the sun for you and me to sail to

I am overboard
the waves are rough
they batter me
and toss me aside
like a piece of driftwood
not wanted
not needed
by you
anymore

I am clinging on
hoping to be rescued
and to be put back on board
the ship
that sails
on the sea of life

S A Hoggand

A HORSEY LAUGH

'Twas late one night upon the farm, when Nellie took our old Fred's arm
'There's sommat goin' on' she said, and pushed him wholly out of bed
'Come on' she said, 'get up - be quick,' and then she organised a kick
Which got him angry as a bear - he fell and missed each bloody stair
And when he reached the hall he cried, 'What's goin' on? I nearly died!'
'The horse is loose!' our Nellie said, and calmly she went back to bed
Fred grabbed his wellies coat and hat, and just in case, his cricket bat
He tip-toed out across the lawn, 'Twas dark an hour before the dawn
He was confused and half asleep, he nearly started counting sheep
But then he saw the stable door was open - it was closed before
'Oh my God the horse has bolted,' Fred woke up, indeed was jolted
Something fell and then he knew - the place he kept his garden tools
'Come 'ere matey boy' he said, and poked his head around the shed
He caught his coat sleeve on a nail, his left boot went inside the pail
There followed an almighty crash, as our Fred broke out in a rash
'You'll never get away from me,' - the pony flicked his tail with glee

If Fred had gone along apace, he would have seen the horse's face
A little animated quirk - a horsey smile? No, just a smirk!

Julia Wallis-Bradford

11

MEALS ON WHEELS

Len looked after the old folk in my Dad's road.
Invalided out of work when he wasn't very old,
he did all their odd jobs for very little pay,
called on them daily to make sure they were OK.

Once when he woke in the middle of the night,
he saw Dad's house all a'glowing with light.
'What's the old devil doing now?' he says to himself,
As he dresses and fetches Dad's key from the shelf.

Crosses the road as quickly as he can,
Is greeted by Dad grasping a large saucepan.
'Comes to something when you've got to make your own lunch,
Those Meals on Wheels people are a right lazy bunch,
it's two o'clock, I've just had a look,
it's a damn good job I know how to cook.'

That he is muddled is plain to see,
Len sits him down and makes him some tea.
Over the hiss of the kettle he hears Dad say,
'If I was in charge they wouldn't get their pay!'

With the patience of a saint Len tries to explain
that it's two in the morning and Dad is to blame.

Sylvia Harris

YESTERDAY

The teachers never noticed
No-one cared to say
What are those weals upon your legs
They weren't there yesterday.

Why are you always by yourself
When we go out to play
What are those bruises on your arms
They weren't there yesterday

Why will they never let you come
To have some tea and stay
My birthday party was such fun
You weren't there yesterday

You always look so wan and sad
As if you've lost your way
But we're quite curious to know
Why you're not here today

Such excitement then at playtime
Kindly lady - hair quite grey
Came to the school and hugged you
Was this just yesterday?

We heard you call her 'Grandma'
We heard her say 'I pray
Forgiveness for not being here
Where was I yesterday?'

We heard she took you with her
To the country far away
And now we know you're happy
And forgetting yesterday

Enid Gill

LOST LAMENT

And so I write a lost lament,
Lost in the darkest chasm five miles down,
Where molten lava bubbles and spits fire in the heart of the earth,
And hell-bound souls roam with infinite torment,
Pleading insanity and praying for ground level,
Where the grass is green,
And the sea breeze cools the hot summer air,
And lawn mowers hum to the tune of the skylark,
How the aroma of freshly cut grass creates such happy childhood visions,
That somehow we lose in the tumultuous years of adolescence and the void,
The void?
The vast emptiness that cannot be filled by time, money or God,
Suddenly, I realise the void is not one, but a thousand empty spaces
crashing around in spiritual pandemonium,
Waiting for their obliterator to take them from the arena and lay them to rest
for all eternity.

Roger Brint

UNTITLED

You told me the girls never wanted a lover,
They never could see you as more than a friend,
Is she aware of your innocent mind?
Will you lead her on to a bitter end?
Who is she this woman who means nothing to you,
How does she draw you if not with her smile?
Does she offer you only a smoke - or a beer?
How does she keep you if not with her guile?

Does her smile touch your heart like butterfly wings,
an innocent flutter of friendship within?
Does she share with you secrets - in confidence,
burnish your ego as she gathers you in.
Do you tell her how wise and kind you are
and how much you love your child?
And how no-one cares enough for you,
how disillusion drives you wild?

Did you tell her how you tore out my spirit,
as once you tore out my heart when we kissed,
and flung it, like flesh to be burnt at your altar
my heart lying crushed in the ball of your fist.
Cowering, shaking, stripped bare to the bone;
white like a pig in the throes of its death
The blade of your ego ripping open its belly,
choked by the stench of the words on your breath.

I once had a lover who lied to his wife;
She looked into my eyes and I looked away,
She didn't look evil, she looked tired of life,
She said 'All men are faithful until they betray.'

Nicola Griffiths

15

MYSTIC MINUTES

As morning mists lift their skirts
Above this green but tortured land,
Then pipers call to quarters
And the men in white raise up their hands
to praise in ancient ritual mime.

When the silver lady spread her arms
and the hunter's horn is blown,
The hornéd beast will lift his head
and a glimpse of truth is shown.
So mystic minutes call to us
Down through the shades of history,
A breath of truth,
A kiss of life,
A whisper in the dark,
An earthly plea to mend a broken heart
to end this bloody sacrifice of
which we all are part.

As the eve of darkness comes,
and we wait to celebrate
with the flicker of a candle,
to bless the symbol of our fate
I wonder if we'll know the truth
or if it's just too late.

Willsong

A DREAM THAT KEPT US APART

I woke disturbed this morning
from another restless dream
I woke disturbed this morning
not knowing what it means.

I woke disturbed this morning
with a thumping in my head
Dartmoor!
I had been crying
for a friend that I thought was dead.

I wanted to walk your bracken hills
to see your sunlit moors
I wanted to listen to the skylark sing
and caress the grass where it folds
I wanted to sit on your granite knee
while I held and hugged the twisted tree
and I wanted to hear your whispering stream
as sweetly it embraces my inner need.

Your pull is too strong - it beats in my head
I have to reach out for the map on my bed
that will show me a maze of long winding lanes
and a spiritual path to the depths of your heart
Once there I can rest -
Together at last

I woke disturbed this morning
from a dream -
that kept us apart.

Jane Ifold

DARTMOOR

Dartmoor, Dartmoor, wild and free,
How strongly you do call to me,
What mood are you in today?
Cold and remote or bright and gay?
You are bathed today in bronze and gold,
Autumn colours, bright, crisp and cold,
Your bracken now all dry and browned,
You still have the beauty to astound.
You have the power to call me to your side,
To you all my secrets I confide
You patiently listen to me,
But you never judge me,
Through the stress and strife,
Of what today is called life.
You alone have stood by me,
Your comfort and support offered free,
My happiness is yours to share.
Because I know you always care.
I live in the shadow of your tors,
And can hear all your sighs and roars.
Dartmoor, Dartmoor, wild and free,
I find peace when I'm with thee.

B Williams

THE JUMPER

I have outlived my usefulness,
Discarded to my loneliness,
Rejected here upon the shelf,
My only company, myself.

It is a dreadful truth to see
To know that no-body wants me;
Of this sad fact there is no doubt,
Who'd want me now, I'm too worn out.

Before me now my life is played
As I sit here with edges frayed,
Each fibre of my being stretched,
My misery in creases etched.

Unravelling, I wonder why
It came to this, I start to cry;
I long for peace in endless sleep,
With eyes closed, off the cliff I leap.

P G S Gibson

SILENT TEARS

I see the pain my little one
I see the pain you feel
I know you hurt down deep inside
I know the pain is real.

You try to work it out I know
You try to sort it out
You wonder what these feelings are
And what it's all about.

Life can sometimes be so cruel
To innocents like you
You don't deserve to feel this hurt
Though I still feel it too.

I try to understand their ways,
I understand your fears
I too try to work it out
When I see your silent tears
Tears that oh! so quietly fall
Tears right from your heart
To ease the hurt and soothe the pain
It makes no sense at all.

You have your rights in this big world
Your right to be a child
To steal these rights away from you
Just makes the whole thing wild.

But one day I can promise you
These silent tears will dry,
And one day when you're older
To understand you'll try.
To make sense of the mayhem
To make sense of it all
Then and only then my love
Will these tears no longer fall.

M Sluggett

20

UNTITLED

My beautiful mother
you're in my heart and soul,
I'm finding it so hard
to let you go,
I know I've got my memories
of things we used to do,
although they are there forever
I'd much rather have you.

It's not been easy
these past two years,
I'm still trying to fight
against these tears.
They said that time
would heal the pain,
How much time has got to pass?
When will I feel right again?

I feel so lonely
lost in a world of my own,
no-one to talk to
I feel so alone.
I'm sat here feeling
so broken-hearted,
thinking about you, mum,
now you have departed.

Sandra Nicholls

OH, WHAT HAVE THEY DONE?

Oh, what have they done to the land that I knew,
To the fields, to the lanes, to the trees?
Why have they taken the colours away,
And killed all the food for the bees?

The buzzing has gone, and the flowers are no more.
The houses have sprung up instead.
The roads are so busy, the noise is so great,
I don't like the sounds in my head.

It used to be quiet, if quiet it was,
When the birds and the bees sang their song;
But now it's so bad, it makes me feel sad
To see how it's all gone so wrong.

People need homes, the experts had said,
With no thought for the views of the sea.
So down went the tarmac and up went the walls,
And the houses were sold with some glee.

But the mood seemed to change when the sights became dull,
And the windows afforded the view
Of more and more houses, and less of the land
And the countryside I once knew.

J Mealing

DREAM COTTAGE

There is a house, it's hidden from view
High on the moor, it's old not new
Trees, hedges, bushes all standing tall
Perhaps there's no room for a cottage at all!

P J Powell

LIFE

A child is born, its hand shut tight.
Not knowing yet what's wrong from right.
It needs just love and tenderness.
A gentle hug a warm caress.
As time goes by he learns to walk.
Then he starts to learn to talk.
Then he learns to read and write
And understand what's wrong and right
Once he starts he grows so fast
Leaving childhood in the past
Soon he's flowing through his teens
Understands what living means
Then he's grown into a man
Living life the best he can
Now he's old time goes so fast
He sits and thinks about the past
His time has come he's passed away
Somewhere a child was born today.

L J Symons

HEAVEN IS A PLACE ON EARTH

Our eyes meet - you touch my heart;
Its broken wings can fly again.
I'm walking on air - I feel so good.
The moon shines, like my love for you.
The stars seem so close as you stand by me.
Then our lips touch: this is my dream come true.
I could stay here forever in your warm embrace.
Without love there is no peace.
The world is silent now.
My love for you grows.
Our heartbeats echo through the streets.
I feel great. You are mine.
As we walk and talk, a glow warms the horizon:
But your smile is warmer than the morning sun,
Time stands still; not a sound to be heard:
But I hear a sound - the sound of love,
Playing its sweet tune to us.

Faye Nunn (14)

WHAT ROAD TO TAKE?

What road to take?
To learn new ways
Or stop a while to rest
To let the memories fade.

Who will guide me?
The path is quite bare
My friends are around me
But you are not there.

So which is the direction?
Which mountain to climb
Before the pastures are green again
And Happiness is mine.

Hazel Nicholls

STORM WATCHING

Silently
the storm closes in
vast shadows of tombstone grey
engulf a stirring sky
above me dances a sky
shrouded in grey menacing phantoms
soon
elegant beads
of dancing rain
knock at my window
cast out by the phantoms
that dance above
I watch as they trickle and fade
into the moor
they are washed away
suddenly
my phantom above me roars his fiendish laughter
echoes disturbing my sleeping moorlands
now he has set his demons of silver free
I watch in silence as they challenge one another
now
the sky is alive disturbed by phantoms
that roar and demons that chase and unease me
they strike at one another in such haste
twisting and tangling casting their haunting
silver light
demons
of the night sky I watch you in silence
until you fade and retreat into your tombstone
grey sky

Sharron Ann Evans

THE CHANGE OF LOVE

Why does my heart not skip a beat
Now when he and I meet
A distance of time has passed since
    we first met
He no longer calls me his pet.
Love is different when you get old
When you are young you should be told
His hair now gone
Weight he's gained
Oh! I wish he would make
my heart beat fast
   again.

Maureen Cogar

NO GOOD?

Life's no good without a goal,
A body's no good without a soul;
A purse is no good without a shilling,
A sandwich is no good without a filling.
A brain is no good without a mind,
Bacon's no good without a rind;
A ransom's no good without a hostage,
A hot dog's no good without a sausage.
A clock is no good without a time,
A lemon's no good without a lime;
A novel's no good without a story,
A win is no good without any glory.
Paper's no good without a pen,
A Bill is no good without a Ben;
A question's no good without an answer,
A ballet's no good without a dancer.
A bride is no good without a groom,
A witch is no good without a broom;
Gossip's no good without a rumour,
Food is no good without a consumer.
A Hale is no good without a Pace,
People are no good without a place.

Claire Ellis

UNTITLED

Little boy look at the moon,
From the window of your room,
And as you sit here on my knee,
Tell me son, what do you see?
As you gaze into the sky,
Do you wish that you could fly,
Or do you see that bright blue light,
As a symbol of delight?
Sending out its heavenly love,
From the sky, so high above.
Do you see a rippling pool
With sparkling water, soft and cool?
Oh little boy, what do you think?
Did you see that bright star wink?
There's another winking too,
Perhaps they're winking just for you.
There's a moonbeam by your head
He thinks it's time you went to bed.
He's come to watch you while you sleep
With all the secrets that you keep.
So, come on son, what will you dream
'Neath the light of your moonbeam?
You can dream of stars that wink
And make the fluffy clouds blush pink
Or rainbows, with their coloured coats.
Or even dream of sailing boats
Sailing on that pool so deep,
Easy son, you're fast asleep.

W Rees

VIOLENCE

The lightning flashed; it strikes his veins and sends his pulses racing,
It's not the thunder that you hear but the miles his horse is pacing
And then the rage, the stormy rage that's taken o'er the temple
That's captured the cavity of his brain; sent sparks across its hidden domain
With coal-black eyes like Hades; hell fire that burns within
And a heart so full of passion, to create some deadly sin.
Beware! Hyperion approaches.

The sound of Thor's heart beats within, a sound of vibrant fury,
Transmitting jolts to Hyperion to make him judge and jury.
Some dark and hidden shroud of gloom surrounds this human vessel
As the horse's hooves dig in the sand; hurtling stones across the land,
Now daggers of rain play evil notes of rhythm on his skin,
Opening pores to let the deadly shadow of Satan in.
You can hear Hyperion approaching!

Don't trespass on his cruel mind, he doesn't see you there
He has no time for pity, and care exists nowhere.
There's blood flowing down in the river my friend, which cascades on
                                                    reaching the falls.
Then between black hills the sun attacks; the horse gallops on with hot
                                                    rays at their backs.
As he flies across miles of blackened gloom, he sees that Hell awaits him.
The scarlet sky of blazing doom envelops the Martian shadow around them.
Hyperion is fleeing.

When driving impulse sends him on, the force sends rocks asunder.
He won't see sunrise in every stride for the Devil, his soul he'll plunder.
Now howling winds beat the canyon, echoing voices fill his ears,
For Hyperion there's no turning back; he's left such a long and terrible track.
As he wanders on aimlessly, solitary, knowing no fear,
Well, the night is pitch; it's not Hyperion you hear.
Not now - for the Echoes call him *S-a-v-a-g-e.*

Henrietta Lee

SOLUS

The lonely climb.
The angry moor.
To march alone.
To seek a door.

Thoughts disturbed.
A restless mind.
To search alone.
No enemy to find.

Everything to lose.
Nothing to win.
To fight alone.
To battle within.

To struggle so hard.
To cause such pain.
To cry alone.
To kill in vain.

The war is over.
The dead piled high.
To stand alone.
To ask to die.

The darkness falls.
No life to dread.
To die alone.
To find the dead.

Steve Hodgins

JESSICA'S CHRISTENING

Today Jess I shall watch you
As you're brought here by the sea.
To a tiny church to be baptised
As your parents were, and me.
I wish that you could understand
This very special day.
When we shall all make promises
To teach the Christian way.

I wonder if you'll smile or cry
When the vicar wets your head.
Or if you'll just be bored with it
And wished you'd stayed in bed.
I shall have so many thoughts
As I see you on your day
And wish for selfish reasons
A tiny baby you could stay.

When you're grown and come again
To this very lovely place
I hope what life has taught you
Will show in a gentle face.
Perhaps you may think about this Sunday
And that you were privileged to be -
Someone who was taught the faith
And been a young girl by the sea.

B Moore

THE LAST LAUGH

Well now John Major who wanted command
How do you cope with your head in the sand
On sad reflection, you're as bad as the rest
All your worst talent comes out at your desk
Do you think of the people who put trust in you
When schemes and intentions you try to push through
Or were we just pawns in a game that you play
Thinking 'I am the boss and I'll have the last say.'
These are the folks with revised expectations
Who'll say 'We're in charge' when it comes to elections.

Ysabel Greenway

THE VIEW FROM THE BRISTOL ROAD

Down to that smallest city below,
Sheltering from Mendip anger
And drifts of snow.
Look down on Biddlecombe,
Snaking in shades of Autumn brown.
Flaking leaves, down, down, down
To the carpet of woody pulp
By the twisting stream.

Beacon Hill to familiar Avalon
Seems like art's secret creation;
Lush green sweeps of a brush unseen
From Twinhills to the Nuclear Power Station.
A Badgerline bus slinks by,
Negotiates the bend.
The shopping done in Bristol,
So near the journey's end.

It seems the wings of paradise unfold
Each time I make my way
Down that newly-tarmacked road.
The levels and silver tracer of Rhynes,
St Cuthberts and the first urban scenes.
How do you feel at this place?
Like me?
As you look out on Bristol channel's
Muddy, yet inspiring sea.
Then ready you should be, to leave behind
The final pinnacle, Nature's Greens.

Come down to Wells
Down, down, to the city of my youth
And teens.

H M Hubbard

YESTERDAY'S FOOTSTEPS

Will you remember walks down leafy ways,
and picnics by the sparkling stream on sunny summer days?
Will you recall a wooded fairy glade, the buttercups
bright yellow and the daisy chains we made?
Will you remember climbing hand in hand,
imagining you've found some strange enchanted land,
of Giants, handsome princes, strong and tall
who lived inside your head when you were small.
Perhaps a melody or some small thing
will stir a memory of songs we used to sing,
Our laughter ringing in the summer air
on balmy days when you were free from care.
I know that there's a woman and a man,
he's known as Grandad, she is known as Nan,
Who will look back in time when you're both grown
and maybe you have children of your own.
They will remember walks down leafy ways,
two little girls and sun-filled summer days.

Margaret Nolan

SAMUEL

He stood in line; with small tin plate
A pitiful longing came into his eyes
Don't let them say . . . 'Too late'
The burning heat and stinging flies

He remembered again the happy laughter
The shaded forest; the flowing stream,
His friends as they splashed in cool, cool, water
Or was it . . . only a dream?

Where were the fields of golden corn
Where he played at hunting with wooden spear
Where were his mother, sisters, brothers?
From his grimy face he wiped a tear.

Food fell at last, on small tin plate
He sank in the shade of a twisted thorn tree
But for Samuel, like others it came too late
He quietly sighed . . . Samuel was free.

He no longer saw the parched earth crying
Mother, sisters, brothers dying
The forest was dappled with muted light
A shelter from sun at noon day's height.

He saw again the corn cobs glowing
By small thatched home the river flowing
His food untouched on small tin plate
Samuel had entered Heaven's gate.

Margaret Snow

BEYOND THE HILL

I looked beyond the tall green hill
and saw the rainbow stark and still
a shaft of stained glass, a lighted arch
a contrast to the cold grey March.

The clouds came quick and covered its face
leaving a cold, dark landscape in its place
the wind blew through me, I felt its chill
but there was a rainbow beyond the hill.

When I was young and sure of right
the world was full of hope and light
there was always time to laugh and dance
to close your eyes and seize the chance.

But time and life can leave their mark
and turn your landscape cold and dark,
sap your strength, break your will
and forget the rainbow beyond the hill.

Stephen Milford

AN ODE TO FIRE

I do not knit and sew
I feed my fire
and watch it glow
Snap, crackle, spit
and flare.
Wood burning hissing
speaking squeaking
Telling tales of
journeys past.

Burning wood has its
own perfume
Apple-sweet
Pine-clean
Oak, burns long
Little smoke
Hear my words fire
I speak too
'Relaxation'
Thank you

Kathleen Harper

OUR SOUTH WEST

Heather stretches, man-made meres;
Trees crouched to earth, wind-gnarled boughs.
Bracken-sided valleys, haunts of deer.
Downward water, brackish, clear,
Through wild beauty of our moors.

Blessed green land, gently spanned
By rolling hills, deep-shaded ways.
Peaceful, generous, pleasant land.
Western winds; soft-moisted-air fanned
Place of ancient country lores.

Cliff-fringed beauty, salted breeze,
Cry of gull and surf-drenched sand.
Rocks of varied hue and form, freeze
Immobile to the pounding seas,
Of these our lovely western shores.

Maureen Sanders

IRELAND

The land of loughs and clean seas
where the fish swim with the greatest of ease.

Countryside untouched by human hands
made by God's great mind.

Never a day comes to an end
without a joke from a friend.

Animals playing with freedom of soul
just running with nowhere to go.

Bracken turning from green to gold
all the grain has been sold.

Peat bogs being dug so deep
summers are nice but winters are bleak . . .

I R Cook

MEANING

If you can understand,
What somebody means to you,
After they have gone,
Never meeting them again,
To have known them and moved on,
Yet always remembering them,
Out of the love of your heart,
Understanding is your middle name.
Yesterday is behind us,
Only now is what counts,
Understand this my friend,
Take the moment and pounce,
Unless you live for now,
Regrets are all you will have.
Nobody lives forever,
Many try but all have failed,
Even the sun will die,
Out in the cold dark void,
Never! Never have regrets.

Sean Charles

THE SEA

The sea laps,
The sea sings,
The sea is never silent.
It roars with rage,
Murmurs with love,
As to the land it's sent.

The sea comes,
The sea goes,
The sea is never still.
Crashing on rocks,
Caressing the sand,
Each rock pool watch it fill.

The sea is green,
The sea is blue,
The sea is black and angry.
Now it is grey,
Now it is clear,
With edges white and frothy.

It warms our shores,
It keeps them cool,
It feeds us from its store.
We sail above,
We swim below,
All this and much, much more
The sea gives us,
But also takes
If it's power you ignore.
So friend, respect
Whilst you enjoy,
Don't break its watery law.

Jill Thorn

LOVE LOST AND FOUND

Journey's end in lovers' meeting
Touch renewed in joy of greeting.
Pain is past - the memory fleeting.

Once our days seemed only drifting,
Then years flowed by ever-swifting.
Eyes meet afresh - spirits lifting.

How was it lost, this love so glowing,
Should we have spoken? Each one knowing
That our reward was not for showing.

Tradition pressed to partners taking.
Love led elsewhere, our hearts forsaking.
Sorrow stoney beds were making.

True love in mind recesses biding.
Young dreams from both life partners hiding
If onlys. But 'twas not our deciding.

Full duties done, without reproaching.
Life's ending now is fast approaching,
Death's secrets soon our footsteps broaching.

Final steps. Soul re-awaking
Love once denied, at last for taking.
Forever beckons, new times making.

Pain now past, the memory fleeting,
Touch renewed in joyous greeting.
Journeys ended.
Lovers
Meeting.

Jane Clews

MINSTER BELLS (WIMBORNE)

Burnished evening sunlight bathed warming fields
As blurs of feeding swallows scurried across an open sky
Instinct majestic in its swooping grace and flow.
A nervous deer froze suddenly
Hewn to granite caution
Whilst nearby bells pealed out their summer carol
And sonorous melody thrilled every silent copse.

Church call hovered like a stationary hawk
Echoing hesitantly past long-dead sculptured knights
And browsing ageing visitors
Whisperingly surprised in studied stained glass window gaze -
Armed only with their lightweight pastel cardigans
Fit for the palely illuminated crypt
And any relic of an idle moment.

The bells toll out like kindly thunder
And a distant pheasant struts with oriental ease
And defiantly shrieks an earnest summons to its mate.

C Korta

GOD BLESS OUR LITTLE CHILDREN

Darlings every one.
With chocolate covered faces
Mischievous and full of fun.

He made them in his image
All gentleness and light,
All innocence and purity,
A mother's heart's delight.

In play they stimulate us
To exorbitant delight.
In sleep we rest our weary limbs
Thankful for the night.

But we wouldn't do without them
Our little bundles of great joy.
For God has blessed our children,
Every little girl and boy.

Julie Corcoran

THE BLINK OF AN EYE

I bade goodbye to my companions,
With loving thoughts they sped me on my way,
Through a long passage was I pushed and pulled,
Angry and protesting, into light of day.

The knowledge I brought with me soon forgotten,
A helpless infant here I was again,
To learn to talk, to walk, to go to school,
This realisation filled my soul with pain.

A different path this time was planned for me,
Mistakes to make, new lessons now to learn.
Year followed year, joy followed pain,
'Til time it was for my return.

Into the light again, brighter than earth's sun,
I asked my friends how long I had been gone,
'You did but close your eyes a little while'
I smiled, my eighty years had seemed so long.

Margaret Bradley

TREE OF LIFE AND NATURE

The tree is old,
Standing in the cold,
All upright and bold,
Its bark worn and weather beaten,
What has it seen and heard in its long life,
Witnessing change beyond recognition,
Its roots deep,
Surviving and thriving, years on end,
While humans die and perish,
Leaving memories to cherish,
What will we do when we die,
No longer able to cry,
Will we be remembered by the tree,
Climbing high to its peak in our youth
Who or what will end its life,
The saw, disease, will it perish in a storm sent
Crashing to the ground,
And like us rot and fade into the ground,
No longer echoing with bird sound.

D L Redman

CORRIDOR

If you stand in the corridor
You can hear the whole world:
Some are crying
Some are dead
Some have strangers make their bed
Some would rather die than wed,
The corridor is widening.

The narrow passage made of stone
Not a cross-section of life
Where the rich and poor don't mix
And the young and old stay alone.

I've got youth on my side.
Take your mind
From underneath your hat
And place it on the table
To be looked at.

The oldest man
Is old but dying
The youngest child
Is young, yet crying;
Those in the middle
Start their sighing
At the rain,
Again.

There is more to life than this
Music's death
Not hit but miss
And love is the single word
That is never to be heard,
Again.

Martyn Ingham

FOR KAREN

Oh my love you are an island, in this stormy sea of strife
A never-ending source of comfort, as we chart the paths of life
And my love you stand beside me helping me when I am lost
As a beacon guides the sailor, though the ship is pitched and tossed.

When my heart is full and heavy you are always by my side,
And my eyes are dim and weary, you will always let me hide
In the warmth of your emotion safe and solid as a stone
You are just the best in life, the gentlest peace I've ever known.

Though the words are slow in coming, and are sometimes left behind
They travel like a mighty river, in my heart and in my mind.
Sometimes surging like the torrent, often trickling like the stream
In my waking hours of torment, in my peaceful sea of dreams.
Always they will give me comfort, though the mist obscures the view.
Written in my heart with feeling is the message 'I love you.'

Jeff Stoddart

A BORROWED ANGEL

She came in to the family, a little angel,
lent to us for just a while.
Golden hair, blue eyes, laughing mouth,
Glowing with life and love to give to all.

She knew about loving, about living
While in pain. She taught us patience,
And facing life when all around us
things looked black and gloom.

Now, she has gone but is not far away,
She's in our thoughts, our work and play,
She left her mark for ever on our lives,
She was our *borrowed angel.*

Marjorie Horgan

SINS OF THE AVARICE

Circle your score, crows hover in the dawn
Watching, waiting, pursuing your move,
Enter the graveyard where you go to mourn
For the lost soul of greed who has everything to prove,

Technical sprites leap out at you,
They dance before your eyes in hypnotic wonder,

Minor subtractions and major additions,
Counting once more to make sure it is right,
Now your dreams transpire alighting transitions
And your counting goes endlessly into the night.

Thoughts trail back to graveyards where
The dead lie, each one looks upward towards
Them but the crow does not notice,

You do not notice the cry of the loved ones,
You do not heed the warnings life,
Too busy fixing, fiddling your own sums,
Too pre-occupied to deal life's strife,

The graveyard will close itself around you
And then you will look to others for the blame,
Perhaps stop your counting but then it's too late,

Beyond and below any pity of mine
Your crow's blood spews its soul,
All I ever counted were the stresses in rhyme,
You've dug your own grave now I'll fill in your hole.

Ah the sins of the avarice.

P C Gooding

FISHERS OF MEN

'I will make you Fishers of Men,' He said
To those fishermen on the Galilean shore,
'Put down your nets and follow Me,
And your life will be worth so much more!'

'Leave your tax collecting,' He said to another,
'To do God's work, to money pay no heed,
Put your faith and trust in the Lord above
And He will supply all your needs.'

Sometimes, the disciples failed and let Him down,
Simple men, unaware of His Heavenly affiliation,
His kinship was outside their understanding
And came slowly to these men of humble station.

One, eventually betrayed this Man of love,
Some slept while He was agonising,
Another denied any knowledge of Him,
While another doubted His rising!

Yet the future of Christendom was left to these men,
First hand they had learnt from the Master,
After His death, they cast their nets out wide,
Their faithful message of truth caught men faster.

Simple truths, steadfast faith, humble men,
Not potential leaders with scholarly minds,
But with Jesus as their teacher and friend,
They spread His message to all mankind.

Pat Heppel

SUMMER THOUGHTS

As I walk around my garden at the start of a new day,
And savour the perfume of the flowers,
And the scent of new mown hay;
I look up at the bright blue sky,
And see the wild geese flying high.
While all around the flowers bright,
Butterflies dance in the morning light.

There is so much beauty in this world of ours
Although man's greed can spoil these happy hours.
In many countries there is war and strife,
With no respect for home or life,
Cruelty to all creatures of God's creation,
Who fight for their lives in every nation,
Starved and beaten and cruelly killed.
No haven for them in this sad world.

But after all is said and done,
It's surely up to everyone,
To help and succour all they can,
For is not that why God made man!

Pamela Martin

TIGER

There's a valley full of tigers
At the foot of Katmandu
Where the sunset on the forest
Lights a sky of cloudless blue
Where the haze of wood smoke lingers
'Neath the trees so strong and tall
Beware the mighty tiger
Most fearsome of them all.

Don't venture from your safe abode
In the forests of the night
For the eyes of stealthy tiger
Are burning clear and bright
Don't think he will not see you
In the gloom of evening light
That his vision will be shrouded
Don't underrate his might

Beware of him he's watching you
You will not hear his tread
His howl carried on the wind
Will turn your fear to dread
Just pray he'll pass and leave you
Mighty hunter of the night
One thing that is certain
He'll kill 'ere morning light.

B E Weaver

THE BEAUTY OF VENUS

A river of rich, dark hair swirled about her face,
unbraided, flowed and curled about her neck,
the scent of honeysuckle, and summer's gentle rains.

Delicate nape exposed, white, unblemished skin,
as cool and flawless as the marble,
upon which she stood.

Eyes the colour of coffee, eddied in
deep pools of sunlight.
Windows upon her soul, not just of sight.

Soft, moist lips parted,
the gentle texture of wild rose.
This tender opening,
never having spoken words,
yet open to so much verse.

Magnificent breast, yielding to the touch,
viewed by so many but open to so few.
Silky skin swirled over a belly,
of such perfection, so flat, so open to temptation.

Her touch would be but the gentle kiss
of a summer breeze.
Her voice, choirs of angels,
perfection in harmony,
So softly spoken but many to rebuke.

Smooth creamy skin of buttocks exposed,
pure curves of flesh, like a river,
silently flows into a field spun of gold.

Radiant in her beauty,
and naked to us all.
Art is never perfect,
merely enhanced by its flaws.

Jonathan Hicks

THE OUTCAST

The north wind does blow and it really is rather cold.
Perhaps it's not the weather, it's just me getting old.
I've wrapped up warm today, you know thick coat and woolly hat,
But I still feel cold and I need another layer's wrap.
My leather boots are fur lined, well mock fur, you know the stuff.
I've had them for years, but now they're looking rather rough.
My coat is ancient, just like me it's had a lot of use.
When people see me coming, they start shouting out abuse.
They call me 'Tramp,' and 'Vagabond,' and plenty of others, I could name,
And some just whisper, 'Oh, isn't it a shame,'
I am the local idiot, or that is what they choose to think,
And when they go on to me I take a little drink.
Meths is my poison, and that's just how it tastes,
But I drink it all down, not a drop can I afford to waste.
My life in shop doorways is unpleasant to say the least,
My life of a human being is more like that of a beast.
But this is my lot, living in the gutter of your town,
If I were a dog at least I could go to Lost and Found.
I'll live and die here hungry, cold and frozen to the bone.
Yes, live and die here hungry all on my own.

Emma Easterbrook

UNTITLED

You've travelled so far
along without I
and I,
along without you
Now our paths meet
and our hearts beat
to a rhythm anew

Together we go
Where?
We don't know
How far?
How long?
'Tis but a song
Together we travel along

So do not pain,
do not fear
and do not shed
a sorrowed tear
For with our hearts
we will go higher
and share our blessed naked fire.

Faye Klenczon

LATE SUMMER'S EVENING

Hot orange sun, fighting day's survival
Reflecting on the sea, shimmering, dancing interrupted by
White tipped waves, tidal.
It's a summer evening, strolling bare-footed on the beach
Blue sky an occasional cotton bud cloud
Feet warmed by the sand, caressing breeze wrapping the body, like a shroud
Gulls shriek, hopping along the water's edge seeming to be ahead all the time
The salt is on the tongue, seaweed is the smell of Neptune's perfume
Life is sublime
Water laps the ankles, cooling playing with the toes,
Retracting too soon
Unparalleled pleasure, gentle day, Nature's tune.

R C S Whear

LIFE WITHOUT YOU

When we first met so long ago.
The bloom of love began to grow.
Your hair shone in the morning sun.
And I knew that you would be the one,
Even though I never knew your name.
You set my pounding heart aflame.

The way your eyes looked into mine.
My heart knew you were sweet and kind.
We went dancing, stayed out till late.
And our kisses were sweet on our first date.
That was ten years or more ago.
You made me happy, as you know.

As I lie here, my heart is weeping.
And God now has you in His keeping.
No-one knows or questions why.
Someone so young had to die.
Now I'm feeling very blue.
My life is empty without you.

For no-one else could take your place.
In a world I can no longer face.
No longer will you have to wait.
So meet me at the pearly gate.
Where we can walk hand in hand.
Together forever in the promised land.

Marlene Weston

MY CHILD

When she was born, I wanted her to crawl,
When she could crawl, I wanted her to walk,
When she could walk, I wanted her to run,
Now she can run I wish
She'd sit quietly with me!

C McGuin

SEASONS

'What time of year do you like best?' The old man asked of me,
And he closed his eyes in deference as he leaned against the tree.
'I love the fields in summer, rip'ning corn and scent of hay,
To see the lark fly overhead and watch the break of day.'

The old man nodded, pipe in hand with still his eyes shut tight,
'Is there any better time,' he asked, 'to stroll the fields at night?'
'I also love the spring,' I said, 'with blossoms in her hair,
That untamed freedom that she spells and her disregard of care.'

The eyelids flickered in recall at the thought of springs gone by,
Of how the petals fell to earth as confetti from the sky.
'The winter has her beauty too - pale moons upon the snow;
Skeleton tress so stark and bare and sunsets long and low.'

'Aye, winter,' he repeated, 'can have her pretty ways
But when one's flesh is ailing it longs for warmer days.'
'The autumn,' I continued, 'has copper-coloured days,
With golden-tinted sunsets and morns of mist and haze.'

'So, tell me lad, which one is best?' The old man asked of me;
'Spring, summer, autumn, winter, which one is it to be?'
'I love them all, I must confess, not one above the rest.'
The old man opened up his eyes, 'It's the autumn I love best.'

'I had my spring in boyhood, heats of summer I once knew,
My heart endured its wintertime when chilling winds once blew.
But the warmth of summer suns and the wildness of spring days
In harmony are blended into autumn's mellowed ways.'

A Bartlett

MY DAUGHTER

My daughter was good when she was small
Now reaching puberty she stands so tall
She borrows my make-up and looks like a clown
And sprays on perfume to knock anybody down.

Her clothes look eccentric and very way out
But dances a *disco* energetically, without a doubt
The interest is there in her hair at last
I no longer need to nag as in the past.

Yes my daughter once so young and behaved
But now if I chastise her she will just rave
Once she would smile to see my face
Now storms from my presence as if in a race.

To try and encourage her to do her homework
Her head is aching and the hands now hurt
To ask for assistance around the house
She is suddenly ill and as weak as a mouse.

Wardrobe and drawers left open and in a mess
The room is untidy as she chooses her dress
But when she plans something special to do
She creeps around her mum and helps me too.

When she wants to tease and tantalise mum
She is clever in humour and has some fun
But I do not mind a little joke and a laugh
As long as she is happy and stays on the right path.

Susan Gerry

THE MOTH

I had not meant to harm you, but I thought that you were something else -
You flew around my head, and settled on my arm,
The whiteness of your wings matching my sleeve,
And I laughed as you fluttered lightly and delicately before me;
We were as one . . .
My mind as bright and quiet-filled as your daydreams of life;
Then you were gone, or so I thought -
Until you stroked my hair, and gently kissed my neck -
And in that one sad moment, I repulsed you - brushing you away -
As if you were something I did not want, or like . . .
You settled on the floor, whole and perfect,
But quite dead, and lost to me . . .
Yet you were mine, and I was yours,
And in that brief, but tranquil moment
We were both at happy peace, each with the other . . .
And then you put your faith in me, but I betrayed that trust -
I had not meant to end your life,
But I imagined that you were something else -
Forgive me . . .

J Margaret Service

SHEPHERD BOY

In a foreign land, in dust and scrub there was a little shepherd boy,
Burning sun, there was little fun and he had never owned a toy.
Herding sheep on mountain slopes, with them he had to roam,
The cloth bag slung on shoulders thin, with his food to eat, alone,
A hunk of bread, a whistle, he played for hours up there,
Sat on a rock amidst the sheep, the melody floating on air.
No fears or tears, sure-footed, the boy lived like this every day,
Calling the strays, each by name afraid they would wander away.
He met with other shepherds in the old wooden hut on the pass,
Wise old sages taught the youngsters, keen and quick to grasp
About their habits, seasons, sheep, then settled in the hut to sleep.
In summer time wild flowers about his feet, he liked to see,
As the sheep grazed he could laze, to watch the humming bees.
Wild creatures came across his path, no danger did he feel,
His large dark eyes quick to see, a tasty, potential meal.
Tourists do not come this way, it's lonely, bare and empty,
He would smile and contradict, of course he said, 'There's plenty.'
It was the only life he knew although the boy was small
Ingrained in him from tender years to be a shepherd, was his all.
So, we leave him on the mountain in warm summer sun,
Whistle, food and shelter, a fortunate boy, he is the one.

Patricia Evans

A PROMISE

An evening I cannot forget!
I called at a house, and there I met
A little lady, so sweet and fair
Sweeter than a rose in June, I do declare!

Her eyes were not that heavenly blue!
But one could see she was good and true
She had spent her life in helping others
We know what that means, we who are mothers

Little lady could I grow to be just like you?
To have lived my life good and true
And only have good thoughts of all around
Then like you my happiness I will have found,
Dear little lady! You have shown me the way
May your help and guidance with me stay!

Rhoda Hamblyn

MY THANKS TO YOU

I owe so much to you my love
in so many many ways
Your goodness and your thoughtfulness
help me throughout each day.

Although you may not realise
you're gentle and you're kind.
Your everything to me in life
a truly wonderful friend.

I love you dear for all your ways
for everything you do,
For the happy years you have given me
I will always cherish you.

My life would be nothing without you
You're the centre of all that I do
My heart is yours my darling
It will always belong to you.

Eugenie Crook

THE FACE

Rare, dark, small but special,
The eyes of wonder that see the world,
The expression of happiness that
        comes every day,
The lily white skin that comes in at May,
The mouth that speaks the wisdom words
The ears that hear the humming birds.

Jackie Ruffin

BOYHOOD DREAMS

Home from school it seems like heaven
To a ravenous boy of only eleven.
Warm stew and potatoes, I have had enough.
Now my favourite walk 'cos the weather is rough.
Goodbye mum I shall not be late.
I rush outside and slam the gate.

Close by the sands of the Norfolk coast,
Where I always like to walk the most.
Crisp air, strong winds blow in my face.
Leaning against it slows my pace.
As the mighty waves crash upon the sands
Numbness and tingling grip my hands.

The spray, what ozone and freshness of air.
The wind plays games with my hair.
I throw a pebble into the sea.
It seems this world is just meant for me.
Such solitude! Better than school I agree,
As I gaze at the horizon across the sea.

Feeling nearer to God I ask what,
When I grow up will be my lot.
Will I travel across this sea
To distant lands where there is much to see.
Where warm sun shines, and palm trees grow.
Until I am a man will I ever know?

A distant bell! Awakened from my dreams.
I must hurry back to school it seems.
Back to studies, to that same old grind.
Time to leave this paradise behind.
The thing I have learned is never to fear.
When searching for God, I can find him here.

V J Snelling

INSIDE OUT

I walked past a window today
And there I was, looking out.
Young, 25,
With coffee in hand,
Wearing a short-sleeved shirt and red tie.
Warm, safe, secure in my job.
Sitting in the office,
Chatting up the girls,
Enjoying my *perks*.
Free lunches in the Management Canteen,
Flying on the company 'plane,
To Europe and the USA.
An insider,
Earning £40K a year
And stock options.

I walked past a window today,
Looking in.
Old, 55,
One free tea a day,
Warm fleecy shirt, no tie.
Cold, unwanted, redundant,
In the open air,
I talk to the birds
And drink away my memories.
Waiting for my next meal,
From the rubbish bins.
Walking in the wet streets
To *the Social* and back.
An outsider,
Taking handouts from the State
And no hope.

Sam Woollard

AUTUMN

When the Summer dies
And Winter threatens a cold embrace
Autumn shows her magnificent face

Leaves that were green
Turn into a treasure of hue
More precious than gold, colours anew

What price the emerald?
When compared to the deepest ruby red
Set with the best in a topaz bed

And the spiritual contentment
Of amethyst and jasper and amber too
Against a sky of sapphire blue

But this treasure must fall
For Winter with cold-hearted malice
Steals these gems for the Winter palace

In a wild, tempestuous spree
Winter plucks these hues so precious
Because, of Autumn, Winter is so very jealous

Each one of us will see Autumn
Like leaves on the ground we will lie
The fact of life is . . . all things must die

Ken Todd

WHISPERS TOO

High in the sky a cloud passes by,
A teardrop falls to the ground below,
In the droplet of water, on the bare earth,
A seedling appears, a wonderful birth,
Growing tall, reaching to see,
Soon it becomes a beautiful tree.
On the branch of the tree, high above,
A bird sits singing, sweet songs of love,
Then off with, to her nest, she flies,
In the midst of the leaves, hidden from eyes.
There sat on four eggs, she patiently waits,
Until in turn each shell cracks and breaks.
Four chicks, beaks opening wide gaze above,
To their doting mother, bringing food, giving love,
Soon from their nest the fledglings will fly,
As high in the sky a cloud passes by.

M A Watts

ONLY YESTERDAY

Wasn't it only yesterday that they were very small?
Now she's become a beauty, he's handsome strong and tall.
Wasn't it only yesterday they climbed upon my knee
I read them tales, we all sang songs, they helped make cakes for tea.
Wasn't it only yesterday they ran along the beach
With buckets, spades and fishing nets
The rock pools for to reach.
It wasn't only yesterday, the years go by so fast
Their future lies before them all I can do is ask
That Lady Luck will smile on them
Good fortune come their way,
My Grandchildren whose childhood was only yesterday.

Gwyneth D Futer

DEATH

When a loved one dies, it's hard to bear
The knowledge that they'll never be there
But a part of them will always be
Inside us - loving us - don't you see

Our loved ones knew the time was near
Death was a release - nothing to fear
But how can they tell us what they were feeling
Would we understand - would we hit the ceiling

It's not something we accept without a fight
We try our best to put things right
We love them so - we can't let them go
Love knows no bounds - don't you know

So maybe we think in time - what is best
There's no longer pain - despair - just rest.

Christine Thain

TOGETHER

We sit together wondering why we are here,
As the sun is setting fast and dark is drawing near.

Colder still it grows, yet warmer seems the night.
Our souls they are as one, our love is free in flight.

You pull me close and then you smile,
Happy we are together, blissful for a while.

I ask how long it will stay like this,
But you answer me only with a tender kiss.

Forever and ever our love will shine,
Never to tarnish with the passing of time.

We'll remember all the happy times that we've had,
All will be peaceful and I'll feel so glad.

Stephen Lubman

THE LOVING FEELING

I can't explain it but I can feel it, something's
telling me you're the one.
You can shatter once fixed emotions like pieces
of broken glass into a frenzy of love and hate
with one touch.
You stroll through my dreams of both day and
night to trespass on personal fantasies and steal
my secrets to the world.
Your face becomes an image in every cloud I see
and your voice rings out in the darkness of my mind.
People say it won't last but when you hold me in
your arms my body tingles with anticipation.
Through my eyes I see the purest picture of
perfection and being without you makes me blue.
When you kiss me I feel that it's too good to
be true and in my heart I know I love you.

N Joy

SAUNTON SANDS, NORTH DEVON

A palette of hues
Of mixed-in colours.
Grasses and dunes form
A metamorphic scape.

Mysterious cries issue
From small visitors
Who come to make magic
In the windy crater.

Sandy soles and gritty hair
Creep home hungry
Dazed by the colours of sound and touch
Left behind until tomorrow.

Eve de Meza

THE LONESOME LIMESTONE HILLS

The openness of the fresh cut fields.
Hearing nothing as one walks on by.
Early morning - hollows holding mist,
Concealing lost forgotten sighs.

Over the rise the sun appearing;
Umbrellas of light speed away the dark
Night's stillness into a distant past,
That's broken by a faraway bark.

Yonder through the still new morning haze,
One figure guides milk carriers on
From fields of pasture to farming byres,
Such daily industry is always done.

Once churns are full and sped away, and
Morning chores finished - children stir,
Emerging onward to education,
Riding away on sleepy transfer.

So the country wakes to daily tasks.
Ever never-ending, year on year.
The life of these farming folk,
Is like the Earth's revolving sphere.

Nothing changes; only the seasons.
Tilling, sowing, reaping the harvest,
Hamlets, villages, every farmyard
Each toils the land till night brings its rest.

What thoughts are held within such farmers,
Earning reward from those fields, dew wet.
Somewhere, on the rolling pastures of -
The lonely limestone hills, Somerset.

David Rossington

TO FATHER

Oh to see you now
small, thin
crying and frightened
one arm not working any more
your speech impaired
lying in the hospital bed
your face unshaved
And yet I know
inside this shell there lives
a great strong man
a proud father
a laughing cheeky boy
a loving son
I comfort you and
cry inside
hold your hand and
give you my love
Our bond is strong.

M A James

VICTIM

She sat, alone
among a pack of hostile girls,
talking, laughing, joking between themselves
but never a kind word to her.

She sat, alone.
Someone walked past
and she raised her eyes in hope of a smile.
She received nothing.

She sat, alone,
alone as always.
She said nothing and nothing was said to her.
But her eyes spelt her feelings.
She was alone, rejected, unhappy.

One day, as she sat alone,
someone spoke to her.
A girl walked past and laughed in spite
and the pack followed.

She sat, not alone,
instead accompanied by spiteful, vindictive chatter.
She sat, her arms folded protectively around her,
saying nothing in return.
She had no power; she was the victim
and could say nothing to defend herself.

I looked towards her and smiled.
She smiled in return and her eyes filled with happiness.

She sat, alone,
alone while they tore at her stability,.
She looked at me as if begging for help.
But I turned away with a bleeding heart
and laughed with the rest.

Alice Paxton

THOUGHTS OF THE BEACH

I'd like to go to the beach today
I fancy a day trip away,
the sand and sea
would be so good for me,
I'd like to stay all day.
I'd swim in the sea
and drink warm tea,
I'd walk along the sandy bay
and all my worries would ebb away,
I would feel so free.
But all too soon the sky would turn grey
and I'd have to go away,
I'd take one last look at the sea
before I came home for my tea,
but promise to come again another day.

Linda Casey

DADDY'S HOME

A father loved his daughter
But possibly too much
You see he walked her room at night
Had fun
Played games he touched
No-one in the house did know
And no-one heard her cry
And no-one saw the pain or guilt
That lay between her eyes
The years went by
And nothing changed
He still walked free and played his games
Her mother she was not to be
Too drunk to care too drunk to see
A little girl nowhere to hide
No mum or dad just tears she cried
Till then that day
She had to leave
No more could she take of her father's deed
She left at sixteen
To the streets she did flee
A little girl lost
Daddy why me?

Lee Robinson

EDITH BROWN

Edith Brown dressed in pink,
What is it you think of
As you walk down Ford Street?
Do you long to be young
Like a certain someone
You just happened to meet?
Did his smile warm you so,
Like one from long ago
That stirred your virgin heart?
Or did your thoughts stray
To a faraway day,
To his oath not to *part*?

Edith Brown dressed in pink,
What is it you think of
As you walk on your way?
Do you think of the night
In your silk gown of white,
He swore to always stay?
Have the years passed so fast?
Does his sweet oath not last
Past the day that he died?
Was his promise too brief,
Or is it just your grief
That makes you think he lied?

Edith Brown dressed in pink,
What is it you think of
As you walk to his stone?
Do you think that you hear
His voice say, 'My dear
You won't be long alone!'

Shelley Jones

GOD'S LOVE

Gazing in my direction
there was a smile.
A warm, happy, fulfilling smile.
A joyful being in the distance
reflecting God's love.

A child, a child of God's
dancing merrily around His world
Proclaiming His truth to man.
His purity, His word,
His love for all.

The smile grows wider as His
love spreads.
His word echoing within His creations
within His world.
His love, as innocent as a child's
protects all His people,
protects me.

Danielle Dovidio

UNTITLED

A distant joy
long forgotten
like a dormant volcano
now kindled, revived
erupts
intoxicating the very air
with a perfume so sweet
the fragrance of spring cannot compare.

Coursing a gorge through the rocks and boulders
erected in defiance of intruders,
this lava of love gently usurps
the coldness of grey stone
and a new heat and hope trickles in
to revive the epicentre of my being.

Not through counterfeit displays of bravado
nor deceitful flattery
do the walls around my heart crumble.
Cruel words of the past
received, and given in return;
scars which once gripped me,
mocking and corroding my foundation,
dissolve
as the portal of life is unbarred
and my tomb is illuminated by the sun's rays.

Deep within this gaping chasm, long existed
a new phenomenon has appeared
melting my frozen heart
and radiating me
in a warm glow
of unreserved love.

Alison Ansell

BUTTERFLY

Delicate fragile wings.
Gossamer woven by fairy fingers,
Embroidered with false eyes
Myriad colours blending
Freed to experience
The strange ecstasy
Of nectar in the bell
Of every flower that blooms.
Precious promiscuity,
Taught by the lazy days
Of summer, sundrenched
And satiated.

Jenny Cox

A BETTER LIGHT

Sunning the valleys
Sweeping the winds,
Dusting the dreams
On life's busy schemes.
Cleaning the world up in a swoop,
Be ready for tomorrow
Leave not a trace,
It's the children's future
Let them see its grace.

P Moon

SPARKY

Now you're gone, our lovely Sparky,
Everybody's friend.
We witnessed all your days and saw your end.
Never a blight
Upon your life down here
Always a pleasure to us in every sphere.

As doggie years are calculated
By those who know
Four-score years you had,
All but a month or two.
Never a moment of that time was spent
Except in happiness and joy
Where'er you went.

You had as many friends as Schulz's Snoopy.
Your antics and responses
Just as loopy.
We enjoyed your frolics and your love,
And wish you luck and happiness where'er you rove

A little pup has come to take your space,
Old Sparks.
He's full of naughtiness and lovely larks.
He lifts our hearts with all his fun and play.
He'll keep us happy as you did here,
For many a day.

His name is Sable,
This naughty little lad,
His feet are big, and as I hear his footsteps pad
I hear you bouncing, joining in the cry and hue.
I hope he'll grow to be
Just half as nice as you!

Thank you Old Sparks, for all you did for us.
Love and friendliness. Obedience. No fuss.

Dymoke Jowitt

THE LITTLE BROWN BIRD

With the demise of the sparrow there is so much sorrow for this tiny brown
feathered bird.
It seems that the bolder, the bigger, the brighter birds are now the ones to
be heard.
It's sad in a way that at start of each day, a few crumbs would suffice the
wee thing.
Now we hear, greedy starlings, the rook and the crow, is nature trying to
tell us something . . .
. . . Such things - that you must be the forthright type, not meek, sedate
or shy.
In today's world it seems that the brash with extremes, are the ones that
will only fly high.
Such a shame when the quieter person is the version that I do approve . . .
. . . is easier to talk to and will sit and listen to, of what troubles the
brash disapprove.

So sorry young sparrow, this world is too narrow, for the meek and the
likes such as us.
We'll live our lives the best way that we can, and the bold will remain
with their push.
We are put in the bracket of mice not the racket of the bigger and
mightier rat.
We are content with our lives and do not surprise, but the rat must
remember the cat.
The cat is so quick, his claws ready to grip the sparrows and rats of
this world.
There is always one stronger as we find as life's longer, but, if we all stay
together and not get oppressed,
I know, and you do, who will come off best.
But, unfortunately not in this case - poor sparrow.

Lucy-May

SIREN OF THE SEA

Sunset, walking by the sea
I heard a voice calling me
Looked around, there's no-one there
Just a whisper in the air.
Wait a while, there it is again!
How's the wind get to know my name?
Silhouette against the sky
Soulful look in tearful eye
On her head a coral crown
Hair of gold tumbling down
Sapphire eyes and ruby lips
A face to stop a thousand ships
Is she just a sailor's dream
Often talked of, never seen?
No, there she is across the sea
Why appear and sing for me?
Is she yet all in my head?
She's beautiful as they all said
No, she's in reality!
She reaches out and touches me
Song so mournful yet so fair
Fixes me in longing stare
Bids me join her midst the spray
How can I let her get away?
And still no-one but I can see
This vision from beneath the sea
Now she comes to take my hand
And walk with me along the sand
My faith in her has broken the spell
Which tied her tight beneath the swell
So now at last she's broken free
To be for evermore with me.

Alan Holt

APPLE JUICE

C ried through the ages
H eart beat too sound,
R easoned with loved ones
I mmersed into ground.
S lowly stopped fighting,
T oo guilty to try.

A dam she's ready
P leasing to sight,
P retty and shapely
E at, swallow the bite.
A nd then you'll blame her
R eap your own hell,
E nter her body
D evil's temple.

F airest of maidens
I mmortal, no skin,
R eason he knows not
S owed seedy sin,
T ore your naked flesh.

T omorrow will blame you,
O ut of mind the sight.

A nd nothing ever changes.

W ake up Deborah!
O h, you led the fight
M ighty warrior.
A nd yet we're still crying . . .
N ever ending story.

Elaine Pomm

A CHILD FOUND

On waking where I stooped to lay,
To the day uncovered with urban gestures,
I went my way with an indifference
That matched the weather's,
Through the town where I was known,
My womb, my cradle, my bed and board,
To a night like no other,
To the child.

It was autumn and tension.
I stopped drinking,
Mother was unwell,
Father broke down and could not work.

I no longer remember
Why I wandered to the hill of lovers,
The grass of childhood's end,
With my hair loose, my blouse unbuttoned,
Giving suck to a forsakened child.

Lee Smith

MORNING

I listened to the sparkling air,
Spellbound by its flair,
Alerted sun rays warmed my hair
And softened morning's frosty glare.
An Autumn day so unprepared
Woke silently and unaware,
Dared smell of Spring and scented wings
Of feathers, hedges and fairy rings.
The morning sky lit mystic blue,
Too high to touch, too fast it flew,
Like Chinese patterns shadows grew,
As easily and beautiful.

Gaille Ellis

ALL I ASK

All I ask is that you listen when I need to voice my thoughts
All I ask is that you offer me your hand when I feel lost
All I ask is that you hold me when the nightmares haunt my mind
All I ask is that you guide me when the right road I can't find

All I ask is your forgiveness if mistakes I sometimes make
All I ask is for your patience when I tend to back away
All I ask is for your loyalty as no more lies can I take
All I ask is your sincerity for I don't believe in fakes

All I ask for is kindness, when the hurt's too much to bear
All I ask is for someone who really truly cares
All I ask is you'll share my dreams and always keep them safe
All I ask is for your love and never ending faith

Yes really all I ask for is *you*.

Gina Kaye

THE COLOUR CO-ORDINATOR

I love the forty shades of green
In black I feel so sleek and lean
Tones of brown are not my colour
In beige and tan I'm even duller

White, not cream, I like a lot
Especially when the weather's hot
A touch of lemon I might make
But sunshine yellow I cannot take

Hot reds, oranges, peach and lime
Are not for me, no way, no time
But purple, lilac, violet too
I like to wear, and every blue

First and foremost I'm best in pink
At least that's what I've come to think
From palest baby to the most shocking
I'm in the pink - hat, dress, shoes and stockings

So keep a rainbow in your heart
When choosing from the colour chart
A wide spectrum of every hue
There is a colour here for you

Kate Everard

GROOM'S LAMENT

I'm a very responsible person really,
If anything goes wrong I'm clearly
The one who's responsible to blame,
Which seems a crying shame;
He's getting on to me again
Because I can't find the curb chain;
He says the rein's not on the bit,
Well, how did I know where to put it;
And now he's lost his end,
It's driving me round the bend;
This dissension among the ranks,
When all I want is a little thanks;
Still, they're not a bad lot really,
Even I can see that clearly;
One thing you'll be sure to bet,
I'll have my own day yet.
Time to tot up for the night,
Hooray, I've got the figures right!
I'm a very responsible person really,
If only *they'd* see that more clearly.

Pippin

LUCIFER'S LAMENT

Seek not to gain your saving grace
praying your prayers to empty space
no-one listens' no-one cares
silence answers all your prayers

Not Allah praising mosque
nor incense wreathed pope
can quench that aching thirst
nor satisfy our old despairing hope

No bells that ring, no Talmud rolls
no chanting priest in jewelled stoles
no Buddhist chants nor anguished moan
can wring an echo from the dark unknown

Look around you, not above
men and women live and love
The single truth since time began
the only hope for man is man

John O'Connell

SILVER CAGE

He knows as he stares
That his spirit is not there
That his soul has gone away
And that nobody cares.

He knows that when he stares
The world's a better place
That somebody loves him
He knows he's so wrong.

Sometimes he locks himself away
Locks himself inside a silver cage
He's got everything
But he needs something else.

Sometimes as he stares
He pretends he does not care
About his emptiness inside
And his wish to be a friend.

But he likes to bc loved
Don't we all?
And his life alone will go nowhere
He will remain staring
Until he can find his soul.

Miri Thomas

THE GARDEN OF CHALICE HILL

There is a garden so beautiful
In an earthly paradise without a doubt,
Resting in the bosom of Chalice Hill
With lovely blossom all about.

Spring waters feed into a well
Sweet and fresh to the taste,
Through the gardens cascade
In never ending haste.

The Tor with Saint Michael's Tower
A lonely sentinel stands,
Overlooking this little Eden
Touched, I'm sure, by mysterious hands.

This little garden was born
Out of Glastonbury's mysterious past,
With Joseph, the Abbey, Arthur and the Grail
The mysteries of its history were cast.

David G Smith

A WALK ALONG OUR CLIFFS

When on a cliff top high -
Almost brushing with the sky
The sea of sapphire blue -
White foamy waves rolling by;
Seagulls calling, squalling
Fish sometimes jumping high.
Across the waves a lone fishing boat goes by
In far distant sight a huge sailing ship.
One wonders how many passengers and crew,
Then silently we doze away,
It is such a perfect day.

Norma Pusey

DUST

There's lots of homes around today,
With troubles by the score.
There's *problem kids* and *problem dads*,
No *caring* anymore!

The children shouting 'What's for tea?'
And leaving Mum in a mess
The centre of each world is me!
'Let's disregard the rest!'

It's not that love does not exist,
Or kids are far too idle.
The problem is, there's too much dust,
On the cover of your Bible!

James Bull

PROBLEMS DEFINED

As vanishing land dissolves from view,
A sense of calm throughout the crew,
As soft white crests, who gently creep,
Caress the blue, so smooth yet deep.

A shoal of silver, reflections glisten,
Not a sound, I sigh, then listen . . .
As silence breaks, a distant clap,
The far off skies are turning black.

The stillness now begins to rock,
As fear strikes down upon my flock,
'Batten down the hatches' the violent wind whirls,
With mighty breakers, the cruel sea swirls.

As lightning cracks a towering mast,
A flash of horror for ships of past,
The crashing post, I let out a cry,
Convinced it is my time to die . . .

Awaking - as we idly sail
Tranquillity and peace prevail,
As life itself is true to form,
A lull before, and after the storm!

Lyn Constantine

WARM IN THE HEART

All around me the leaves fall to the ground,
The air is sweet as blackberries.
Although the strength of the sun is failing
It is still warm in the heart of me,

Sometimes the days pass like seconds,
And I wonder how long it will seem
Until I am old and full of stories,
And my body punishes me for the years,

Yes, another year is passing,
It was coloured and flavoured with people and places,
And lessons, all rich and full, and spicy,

And now I feel Your breath - sweeter than blackberries -
Gently blowing the dead leaves from this tree,

Winter may be on its way,
But it will remain warm in the heart of me,
For at the heart of me is You.
And time passes, the seasons change,
But You, my God, are eternally the same.

Tim Sutton

FLY THE RAG

I have no bulldog pride
No stiff upper lip
I see no hope or glory

Fly the rag
red white and blue
fly the rag
of whitewash and lies
burn the flag
it smells of corruption

I have no Dunkirk spirit
I see no Jerusalem
no green and pleasant land
just Britannia drowning at sea

Fly the rag
red white and blue
fly the rag
of secrecy and hypocrisy
burn the flag
it smells of arrogance.

Geoff Downton

DISCOVERY

There's friendship in the river's gentle power,
        Majesty in the great, unbounded sea,
Creation in a flower,
        Grace in a swaying tree.

There's beauty in a tender, precious name
        And treasure in a book,
Art in every game,
        A sentence in a look.

There's freedom in the wild wind's restless play,
        Simplicity in a thought profound,
Gladness in colour gay,
        Music in every sound.

There's timeless wealth in a memory that does not wear,
        Innocence in a baby's eye,
P'raps sorrow in a tear,
        Courage in a radiant smile.

There's triumph in a field of harvest corn,
        Resurrection life in love Heaven giv'n,
Hope in every dawn,
        Joy in living.

There's peace to be found in a garden fair,
        Expression in the artist's skilful pride,
Sacrifice in care,
        Rhythms in the tide.

There's crystal-brilliance in a drop of dew,
        Fragrance in a deed that's kindly done,
Gold in friendship true,
        Glory in setting sun.

Mavis Sutton

ILFRACOMBE IN MARCH

A smoky haze hangs over the sea . . .
The softness of colour reaches out to me.
Spring in its beauty . . . the balmy air,
Colours exquisite without summer glare.
The soft splash of waves on the incoming tide
Memories of holidays will always abide
As I gaze in admiration at the rugged coastline
And I realised the longing was always mine -

The sea is glistening in a beauty so rare
Beyond all doubt none can compare
The mystery it holds is beyond belief . . .
All troubles resolved - no time for grief.
With the peace and contentment inspired in me now
I know that I answered a call somehow!
I must share my good fortune in some small way
As I thank God for each new day.

A Joan Hambling

FLOTSAM 'N' JETSAM

Sea blown, wind blown,
God what have we done?
Plastic 'n' cans
Buts of nets and broken bottles
Jagged in their edge.
Makes you think
God what have we done?

Look at the litter strewn,
Birds oiled in decay,
Flotsam 'n' jetsam
Fancy names for our fancy rubbish.

Huge trees somehow coughed up and regurgitating
Spilling out the tide
Like an elephant's skull from an elephants' graveyard,
Gnarled to their touch, telling of a different story.

Sea blown, wind blown,
God what have we done?
Plastic 'n' cans
The scatter and they run across the sands.
Flotsam and jetsam
Fancy names to our fancy rubbish.

God said that it was good,
God what have we done?

Andrew J Fry

THE TRAVELLER

When the noise and bustle of day is over,
And the peace of the night is here,
The comforting silence closes around,
Like a friend that is ever dear.
And the moon like a lantern lights the way,
And the stars are the tears of the day,
So, I settle down now in my favourite armchair,
Till, tomorrow, I go on my way.

B May

MOTHS

Blue meteors between the apple trees;
Crisp as dead leaves, they blur
On a mercury vapour, lay their model
Plane shapes on the phosphorescent sheet,

Or fumble on a glass rim thick
With ether and malt-sweet
As the drowsy breath of a
Mother's kiss. The last flicker of

Tired eyelids; grey charcoal stains;
Moths pinned in descending boxes,
Their furled-up husks flaking like
Snapshots; and dust-colourless.

Paul Davidson

THE MYSTERY? HIS SHADOW

A little boy next door to me.
He's three or maybe four.
One evening at the close of day
I watched him from my door.

He laughed, he jumped, he ran, he played
With his shadow on the ground.
When suddenly the sun went in,
It was nowhere to be found.

He sat upon his back door step,
His head held in his hands.
Just where his little friend had gone
He couldn't understand.

I ran and took him in my arms
To explain the mystery.
'Oh! Lady, lady, I miss him,'
He said so quietly.

But how could I explain to him
That tomorrow is another day,
That hopefully the sun will shine
And again with his friend he will play.

Sheila Braund

THE GIVER'S GIFT

'The cat has done a runner,' I was informed by my son.
Trust her, on a cold winter's night, but as she's the oldest one
I knew I'd have to look for her and that I'd be alone,
'Cos everyone else was out and Dave was on the phone.

Begrudgingly, I pulled on my coat and trudged up the street,
Right to the end where the woods and houses meet.
I tripped on the slope that led down past the laden trees
And landed in an area where the local dogs pee.

As I staggered to my feet, uttering profanity,
And brushed off my clothes, pondering my sanity
I suddenly became aware that the world was white,
Silent, still, with a moon so bright.

The snow was crisp and powdery, crumbling underfoot.
The trees glistening sculptures, mute witness to the owl's hoot.
The sky was clear, every star twinkling,
As I brushed against the fence, I set some icicles tinkling.

I was enchanted, I must have stood there for an hour.
I felt the same when I opened my door one day, and found a
solitary
sunflower.
God had left me a gift, a thank you for trying.
I found the cat, started home . . . and found I was crying.

Linda Miller

THE TREE

We walked away our summer, we laughed and kicked our heels,
happy in our little world of woods and cliffs and fields,
one day as we were walking, you stopped to look around,
and then picked up an acorn, that was lying on the ground.

You put it in your pocket, I remember it so clear,
both of us so happy that the other one was near,
you put it in the garden, you planted it with pride,
we stood and laughed, the two of us, lovers side by side.

Sure enough, it raised its head, although its pace was slow,
it grew a symbol of our love, as years' time slowly flow,
Autumn came and with it came a peaceful world so gay,
we raised a healthy family and sent them on their way.

The tree still cast its blessing, in sunshine there was shade,
and there upon the lowest branch, we hung the swing we made,
we sat and planned our future, laughing at our plans,
a couple quietly talking, just lovers holding hands.

Winter came with parting, for you have gone away,
you are bound for paradise and I alone must stay.
I sit here in our garden, gazing at your tree,
remembering all the lovely things you ever said to me.

I know that I will find you, the tree it speaks your name,
and when my time to go is come, I'll hold your hand again.
I waken from my dreaming, I look and see you clear,
you've come to take me home with you, I call your name so dear.

You stop and smile so softly, offering your hand,
I take it and kiss it for I've found my promised land,
we turn to go, I stop you, we look back at the tree,
and sitting, seeming, sleeping, is a person that was me.

Dev Deverell

I BELIEVE

I believe in the heaven above
I believe in God's love
and whilst on earth my thoughts do stray
I know that He will show the way
He blesses the poor, the rich and the meek
in sickness and in health His hands do
reach, His help is there for you to ask
and He will answer in His own way.
All you do is put your hands together and
pray, and thank God that He is there to
listen to your little prayer. I thank God, the
Father, and Jesus Christ the Son, the Holy Spirit,
And Mother Mary, the chosen one, the twelve
disciples who were chosen too and my
Guardian Angel who chose me too.

Olivia Audrey

A TRIBUTE

The water, lungs filled,
Black pebbles, grit.

Exhume the dead
And praise all who see them
After all we fish in wooden coffins
Rising, falling on oceans
Fit for no man

The sea requests us to leave
but we do not listen

The earth throws out charcoal ashes
Fiery heat, tornadoes, houses fall
Rubble heaped on tiny fragile bodies.

Men in the city
Count the cost
Damage limitation exercises

PR, PA, Presentation, Packaged

A roomful of grief - stricken women
await the verdict.

Gea Jones

WIND O'ER THE MOORS

As I lie a'bed a'listening,
To the gale that comes a'whistling,
Tearing at the window panes,
Screaming down the narrow lanes,
At least to reach the open moors,
On its way to fight the tors.
Over ponies in a huddle,
And the sheep the ground they cuddle.
At last it meets those mighty stones,
In its fury round them it moans,
But now its strength is nearly spent
Gently now it makes its way,
To greet the dawn, another day!

Patricia Arnold

TIMES PAST

Tell me a story,
Be it short, be it long,
Of days that are over
Of days long gone.

Tell me a story,
Of the places you saw,
And what it was like
In that terrible war.

Tell me a story,
Of people you knew,
Friends and relations
Constant and true.

Tell me a story,
Of the man that you wed,
Was he gentle and caring
Especially in bed.

Tell me a story,
Was he one of the best,
And did you love him
Above all the rest.

Tell me a story,
Of your children you fed,
In an age when babies
Were born home in bed.

Tell me a story,
The tears that you shed,
When living was hard
And so quickly dead.

Tell me a story,
Of what made your past
Full of adventure,
Please make it last.

Tell me a story,
Of the times gone by,
And make the pictures
Dance in my eye.

Tell me a story . . .

Tell me a story . . .

J B Crabb

PIGEONS

Pigeon racing is the thing,
Watching your bird come flying in
When they perch inside their shed
Your hands start shaking and so does your head.

You then take hold of that bird within
Taking that rubber and clocking it in
Now you can sign, with pride and glee
As you wonder if you're first in.

As you sit there on your chair
Looking up into the air
Wonder or not if you'll see some more
Watching out for just one more.

Waiting and watching so patiently
Jumping up at the sight of a bee
Looking out beyond the clouds
Corn in hand you look so proud.

As the day comes to an end
You wonder or not if you'll see them again
In the morning when you get out of bed
Your favourite bird is waiting on the shed.

Although you know losses will occur
You can't stop worrying about your birds
When you know they're home and safe
You can relax until the next race.

Susan Davies

LOST IN DREAMS

The mist goes rolling over me
Covering my eyes, I cannot see.
Like the sand on the shoreline.
The sea - covers me.
Is the time past for glory.
Look into the past, what do you see?
In the visions of the future
Where wild birds fly, do you see me.
Are there really rose-coloured glasses
Or is it just how we see.
There's gotta be a time for glory.
A time to dream.
And the pain, is it passing
In a play, a changing scene.
Are we making our way forward.
Or are we just lost in dreams.

Stuart Noon

TITHES FOR VICAR JOHN - 1268

From dawn to dusk we toil and strive,
For scare enough to stay alive,
Yet decimam partem we must give
Per annos singulos as long as we live,
Whilst Abbot and Vicar thrive.

Shillings and pence from parish oblations,
Beatae Marie Purification,
Our Holy Church's dedication,
Confessions, sponsalium, altar bread,
Sepulturarum of the dead.
Flax, wool, honey, ten shillings of cheese,
Tithes of calves, lambs, foals and geese,
A quarter of barley, fine wheat and fabarum,
Cows, hemp, oats and columbarum.

Twenty five shillings of parish pomorum,
Three and six of porcellorum,
Tithes of all molendinorum,
But that quod vocatur Kockesmille,
Whence all goes to the Abbot still.
Hay from Richard Maloysel,
Monies from *Heypeni* as well,
Thirteen pounds, two shillings, eleven pence
De cuntis fructibus from this day hence.

From dawn to dusk we toil and strive,
For scarce enough to stay alive.
Yet decimam partem we must give
Per annos singulos as long as we live,
Whilst Abbot and Vicar thrive.

Jennifer Bailey

EARTHLY SAINTS

'Who are those ladies of the lamp
who hide behind the scenes?
don't look for notoriety
or medals like the OBE's.
They are the Saints who do so much
to help the sore distressed;
and work so hard for no reward
but only wish to serve the Lord.'

K D Smith

UNTITLED

Animals, animals, when will man learn,
at the moment it's none of their concern,
just torturing and giving animals excruciating pain.

Aches and pains, I can feel flowing round my body.
Someone free me, someone save me,
I need love, attention and plenty of affection.
I'm not just one of man's many collections.

Carol Paine

I ONCE HAD A RELATIONSHIP

I once had a relation-ship,
  But she sailed far away,
Up anchored and set course to find
  Another sheltered bay.

Our stormy and tempestuous affair
  Had ended, sunk at last,
The current which pulled us apart,
  Had run so strong and fast.

She didn't even wave, but left me
  At low ebb, high tide,
Her face was stern, my head was bowed . . .
  My salty tears to hide.

My flag, alas, she flies no longer
  From her stately mast,
Our swell affair was present tense,
  But sadly now it's past.

She left full speed ahead, her sails
  A'billowing like a cloud,
If happiness equals silence,
  My heartbreak's cannon loud!

I stare from port, my eye on a star,
  Bored, like a boat without rudder,
My emotions beached on a lonely shore,
  Left to flounder and shudder.

A vessel like her will shore-ly land
  Another love-struck fool,
I'm only one fish in a big big sea . . .
  And her heart is fathoms cool!

Clive Blake

PROGRESS

What has happened we all ask
to this green and pleasant land
The country lanes where once we strolled
are needed for cars we now are told
The hedges once so filled with flowers
nuts and berries and wild rose bowers
are cut right back and sprayed with goo
Small wildlife lost their safe homes too
Of course they didn't produce big money
Like working bees who provide honey
So out you go, cut down the trees
Make wider roads, pollute the seas
One looks with alarm at damage done
By vandalous powers that be
They turn a blind eye it seems to me
To things that don't produce a fee

Money's the God they all seem to worship
People don't matter, they're expendable, see!

E V Ware

INFORMATION

We hope you have enjoyed reading this book - and that you will continue to enjoy it in the coming years.

If you like reading and writing poetry drop us a line, or give us a call, and we'll send you a free information pack.

Write to

Anchor Books Information
1-2 Wainman Road
Woodston
Peterborough
PE2 7BU